Environmental Management Needs for Exploration and Exploitation of Deep Sea Minerals

ISA TECHNICAL STUDY SERIES

Technical Study No. 1
Global Non-Living Resources on the Extended Continental Shelf:
Prospects at the year 2000

Technical Study No. 2
Polymetallic Massive Sulphides and Cobalt-Rich Ferromanganese Crusts:
Status and Prospects

Technical Study No. 3
Biodiversity, Species Ranges and Gene Flow in the Abyssal Pacific Nodule Province:
Predicting and Managing the Impacts of Deep Seabed Mining

Technical Study No. 4
Issues associated with the Implementation of Article 82 of the United Nations Con-
vention
on the Law of the Sea

Technical Study No. 5
Non-Living Resources of the Continental Shelf Beyond 200 Nautical Miles:
Speculations on the Implementation of Article 82 of the United Nations Convention
on the Law of the Sea

Technical Study No. 6
A Geological Model of Polymetallic Nodule Deposits
in the Clarion-Clipperton Fracture Zone

Technical Study No. 7
Marine Benthic Nematode Molecular Protocol Handbook
(Nematode Barcoding)

Technical Study No. 8
Fauna of Cobalt-Rich Ferromanganese Crust Seamounts

Technical Study No. 9
Environmental Management of Deep-Sea Chemosynthetic Ecosystems:
Justification of and Considerations for a Spatially-Based Approach

Environmental Management Needs for Exploration and Exploitation of Deep Sea Minerals

ISA TECHNICAL STUDY: No.10

International Seabed Authority
Kingston, Jamaica

NATIONAL LIBRARY OF JAMAICA CATALOGUING–IN–PUBLICATION DATA
International Seabed Authority
    Environmental management needs for exploration and exploitation of
deep sea minerals : report of a workshop held by the International Seabed
Authority in collaboration with the Government of Fiji and the SOPAC Division
of the Secretariat of the Pacific Community in Nadi, Fiji, from 29 November to
2 December, 2011
        p. : ill. ; cm. – (Technical study; no. 10)
        ISBN 978-976-8241-04-7 (pbk)

1.   Ocean mining – Environmental aspects
2.   Marine mineral resources – Law and legislation
3. Environmental monitoring
I. Title   II. Series
333.916416   · dc 22

Copyright © International Seabed Authority 2012
International Seabed Authority
14-20 Port Royal Street
Kingston, Jamaica
Tel: (876) 922 9105, Fax: (876) 922 0195
Website: http://www.isa.org.jm

Cover image: An example of a seamount subjected to bottom trawling.
© National Institute of Water & Atmospheric Research Ltd (NIWA)

Contents

List of Acronyms

ACP	African, Caribbean and Pacific Group of States
CBD	Convention on Biological Diversity
CCFZ	Clarion-Clipperton Fracture Zone
CSIRO	Commonwealth Scientific and Industrial Research Organisation
DSM	Deep Sea Mining
EEZ	Exclusive Economic Zone
EIA	Environmental Impact Assessment
EIS	Environmental Impact Statement
EMP	Environmental Management Plan
EMS	Environmental Management System
EU	European Union
FAO	Food and Agriculture Organization
GHG	Greenhouse Gas
IOC	Intergovernmental Oceanographic Commission
ISA	International Seabed Authority
ITLOS	International Tribunal for the Law of the Sea
IUCN	International Union for Conservation of Nature
LOSC	Law of the Sea Convention
LTC	Legal and Technical Commission
NORI	Nauru Ocean Resources Inc
PICs	Pacific Island Countries
PICT	Pacific Island Countries and Territories
REE	Rare Earth Elements
SIDS	Small Island Developing States
SPC	Secretariat of the Pacific Community
SOPAC	Applied Geoscience and Technology Division of SPC
TOML	Tonga Offshore Mining Limited
UNCLOS	United Nations Convention on the Law of the Sea
UNGA	United Nations General Assembly
UOS	University of the Sea

Executive Summary

The International Seabed Authority (hereafter referred to as the Authority) in collaboration with the Government of Fiji and the SOPAC Division of the Secretariat of the Pacific Community (SPC) held a Workshop on Environmental Management Needs for Exploration and Exploitation of Deep Sea Minerals, in Nadi, Fiji, from 29 November to 2 December 2011. This initiative reflected the increasing interest in and associated concerns about the potential environmental impacts of deep sea minerals exploration and mining and how competent authorities at the national and international level will regulate this emerging economic development opportunity in a sustainable manner in areas within and beyond national jurisdiction. The workshop was organized to raise awareness of the nature of the mineral resources found in the seabed in areas beyond the limits of national jurisdiction ("the Area") and on the outer continental shelf. Another objective of the meeting was to assess the measures taken by the Authority with respect to the protection of the marine environment from the harmful effects of deep seabed mining and the applicability of such measures to the development of marine minerals in areas within national jurisdiction. The outputs from the workshop included a draft template for an Environmental Impact Assessment (EIA) of deep seabed mining; an outline of the legislative and regulatory provisions that should form the basis of environmental management of deep seabed mining; and the identification of capacity-building needs and methods by which these needs could be addressed. This document contains the outcomes of the discussions at the workshop.

Statement by Dr. Russell Howorth

Director, SOPAC Division, Secretariat of the Pacific Community

I would like to warmly welcome you all to this International Workshop on Environmental Management Needs for the Exploration and Exploitation of Deep Sea Minerals that is hosted by the Fiji Government and jointly organized by the International Seabed Authority and the South Pacific Applied Geosciences Commission (SOPAC).

A special welcome goes to the Secretary-General of the International Seabed Authority, His Excellency Nii Odunton and his staff who are here with us today. Secretary General, I am aware you were present here in Fiji to attend the Authority's Workshop on the Development of a Geological Model of the Polymetallic Nodule Resources of the Clarion-Clipperton Fracture Zone (CCFZ) in 2003. I believe your presence here today in this workshop signifies the Authority's commitment to supporting Pacific Island Countries (PICs) in their endeavour to fully participate in the exploration and exploitation of seabed mineral resources in the Area, in addition to their aspirations to realize the benefits of developing seabed minerals that occur within their Exclusive Economic Zones (EEZ).

Please allow me to say a few remarks on recent developments relating to deep sea minerals. In doing so I must thank the Secretary-General of the International Seabed Authority who, together with Ambassador Peter Thomson, Fiji's Permanent Representative to the United Nations and the current President of the Assembly of the International Seabed Authority, drove the initiative to convene the workshop in this part of the world. This workshop has particular significance to the region for a number of reasons.

- 2011 is the first year in which the EU-funded SPC SOPAC Division Deep Sea Minerals Project is being implemented in 15 Pacific ACP States and it is vital that the SPC as the implementing agency establish the necessary linkages with regional and international players of this new and emerging industry.

- The issuance of a mining lease to Nautilus Minerals Inc. in Papua New Guinea in January this year is a milestone achievement and has set the pace for the first deep sea mining in the world to be realized in our region.

- Following the Advisory Opinion issued by the International Tribunal for the Law of the Sea (ITLOS) in February 2011, the Council of the International Seabed Authority in July 2011 approved plans of work for exploration in the Area to two companies that are being sponsored by two developing countries, more specifically PICs. Nauru Ocean Resources Inc. (NORI) is sponsored by Nauru. Tonga Offshore Mining Limited (TOML) is supported by Tonga.

- I am sure we will hear during this workshop that other Pacific Island Countries (PICs) have expressed their interest in submitting applications to the Authority for exploration licences in the reserved areas of the CCFZ.

- The recent interest in rare earth elements (REEs) at the global level, and Japan's recent announcement of REE deposit discoveries on the Pacific Ocean seabed has certainly raised eyebrows in the region and PICs are keen to know more about the REEs potential that may occur within their respective national jurisdictions.

- Whilst this emerging industry is expected to commence operations in the region in the near future there remain many unknowns associated with deep sea minerals. These were discussed and a proactive way forward for the region was decided at the High-Level Inaugural Meeting for the SPC SOPAC Division Deep Sea Minerals Project in Nadi in June 2011.

- Whilst there have not yet been adequate studies to determine the potential impacts of deep sea mining on the ocean floor and ecosystem, scientists have begun describing what the impacts might be to help regulators and the public better understand the potential impacts of this new industrial activity on the ocean.

As the region prepares itself to venture into this new industry, I would propose that we move forward with great caution to ensure that we do the right things to protect the interests of our people and future generations. In the June 2011 Deep Sea Minerals Project

workshop, the application of the precautionary approach concept in offshore mineral development came out very strongly and was agreed to as a sensible guiding principle to this new industry. With that in mind, we need to ask what the precautionary principle really means in the context of deep sea mining. I am sure this concept will be a topic of discussion in this workshop not only in defining the precautionary approach concept but also in determining how we are going to make it happen within and beyond the national jurisdiction.

There are various relevant references in the United Nations Convention on the Law of the Sea (UNCLOS) in this regard and I urge that they be brought to the fore during this workshop. One in particular comes to mind, and I quote:

"States shall, directly or through competent international organizations ... provide appropriate assistance, especially to developing States, concerning the preparation of environmental assessments".

It strikes me that the workshop is itself a great example of States doing just this. With those remarks, I would like to once again welcome you all to this workshop.

Thank You.

Statement by the Honourable Minister Timoci Natuva

Minister of Works and Public Utilities, Fiji Government

Having been accorded a traditional welcome in the Fijian manner, allow me now to welcome you on behalf of the government of Fiji to this Fiji, and to this workshop. You have traveled from around the region and indeed from as far away as Jamaica for this workshop, and I am certain that this reflects the interest within our Pacific region in pursuing this emerging opportunity of deep sea mining.

It is a privilege indeed for me to open this workshop, given that deep sea minerals exploration and exploitation is an issue attracting much international attention at the moment, and given the lead role that our region is taking in the global arena, with entities sponsored by Tonga and Nauru becoming the first Small Island Developing States to be granted licenses through the International Seabed Authority this year.

On behalf of Fiji's government, I would like to express in particular our happiness at being able to host this workshop, as an effective means of complementing our role as President in office of the ISA Assembly in the person of Fiji's Permanent Representative to the UN, Fiji's membership of the ISA Council, and the successful election of Fiji and the region's nominee to the Legal and Technical Commission, Dr Russell Howorth, Director of the SOPAC Division of the SPC, who is here today as one of our co-organisers.

We hope that this workshop will continue to build on the momentum created by the issuance of the exploration licenses to Nauru and Tonga and Fiji's leadership of the ISA to address the myriad of issues that are brought to the fore with regard to the requirements for sustainable exploration and extraction of deep sea minerals, both within the EEZs and Extended Continental Shelves of our countries, and in the areas of the oceans under the ambit of the ISA in the Clarion-Clipperton Zone. We have certainly broken ground this year not only with the issuance of licenses to Nauru and Tonga, but also with the advisory opinion from the International Tribunal for the Law of the Sea on the responsibilities and obligations of sponsoring States.

It is worth reiterating here the importance of the resources of the oceans to our small island States in the Pacific, arguably more so than for any other region or State in the world. Our countries collectively control an area 70 times larger than our landmasses. Add to this the possibility of exploiting oceanic resources in the high seas, and the wealth of the oceans cannot be denied, particularly given that our land-based resources are in comparison very limited, and where existing unequally distributed across the region.

This brings to mind Epeli Hau'ofa's depiction of Oceania as a Sea of Islands rather than 'islands in a far sea', with a wealth of ocean resources binding us together and giving us the potential to prosper economically in a holistic manner. We must treat the ocean with the respect accorded to it by all our cultures, and exploit the opportunities deep sea minerals have to offer to the full benefit of our countries, taking into account not just the economic and financial benefits but the socio-economic and indeed environmental considerations that will factor into our decisions.

Your workshop will address a number of issues relating to the exploration and exploitation of deep sea mining opportunities. You will examine the opportunities both within EEZs and within the area controlled through the ISA, concerns relating to the preservation of marine biodiversity and environmental impacts of deep sea mining, the sustainable exploration and exploitation of the resource for maximum economic benefit, and the legal requirements of regulatory frameworks and the precautionary approach in the absence of such frameworks. These are all very technical and detailed issues which will need to be considered individually, and together, for each of you to determine what is in the best interest of your State.

On this note, on behalf of the Government of the Fiji, I would like to acknowledge the assistance rendered by the EU – DSM Project run by SOPAC-SPC to the PACP countries in the convening of the deep seas mining workshops in June and October, and indeed in organizing this workshop. No doubt the results of this workshop will provide further direction to our technical and legal advisors at the DSM project on the needs and priorities of each of our countries.

Together with the ISA's expertise and institutional knowledge which will no doubt be shared with you, I have no doubt that this workshop co-organised by the ISA and SOPAC-SPC will answer all your questions and provide the necessary information to make informed decisions on policy, legal frameworks, and objectives in the area of deep sea mining. On behalf of the government of Fiji, but also if I may take the liberty of speaking on behalf of the participants from the region, I would like to thank the ISA and SOPAC-SPC for all the preparatory work to ensure a rich programme for this workshop, and all the logistical arrangements that allow us to be here in this room together for this workshop.

I would like to leave you with the humble suggestion that you take as a starting point that perspective of Oceania focusing on the wealth of our "Sea of Islands", and our desire to see its rich resources to also sustain future generations of Oceania.

Vinaka Vakalevu.

Statement by Nii Allotey Odunton

Secretary-General, International Seabed Authority

Honourable Minister, I would like to thank, through you, the Government of Fiji for receiving us here and for the warm welcome that it conveyed to us. I particularly wish to thank your cabinet colleagues for the decision to provide all that we needed for this workshop.

May I take this opportunity to recognize the contribution of the South Pacific Applied Geosciences Commission (SOPAC) for its cooperation in organizing this workshop. I wish to congratulate the Director of SOPAC, Dr Russell Howorth, who replaced Isikeli Mataitoga as a member of the International Seabed Authority's Legal and Technical Commission (LTC) on his recent election as a member of the LTC for a five-year term from 2012-2016. His participation in the Commission's work following his election at the recently concluded seventeenth session was appreciated by his colleagues and certainly by the staff of the Authority. On behalf of the Authority, I also wish to thank Dr Howorth and his team from SOPAC for making the local preparations for this workshop.

Distinguished guests, ladies and gentlemen,

This is the thirteenth workshop held by the Authority and the second that we have held here in Fiji. For those of you who have worked with us before, we have appreciated your involvement in our work over the years and it is good to see you again. For those of you that are new to the work of the Authority, I hope that this is the beginning of a fruitful relationship. The Authority's workshops are essential to its work as they provide the necessary background information on the subject matter under consideration, which, among other things, provides its organs with the technical and scientific basis for the formulation of rules, regulations, procedures and recommendations for the conduct of activities in the Area. They are also useful for participants as they provide them with a forum for the exchange of information and ideas.

The International Seabed Authority was established by the United Nations Convention on the Law of the Sea (UNCLOS), and the Agreement relating to the Implementation of Part XI of UNCLOS. Up until the beginning of this year, eight contracts for the exploration for polymetallic nodules had been issued by the Authority. This year alone, four more contracts have been issued, two for polymetallic nodules and two for polymetallic sulphides, hopefully the first of many. It is especially encouraging that the two new contracts for polymetallic nodules come from organizations within this region, highlighting the opportunities for PICs to participate in the exploration and possible further exploitation for marine minerals beyond national jurisdiction.

We are entering a new stage in the development of marine minerals and consequently in the work of the Authority. On the demand side, metals such as copper, nickel, manganese and cobalt are rising steadily; at the same time the environmental requirements for land-based mining are rising concomitantly as well. With regard to environmental regulation for seabed mining, the Authority has taken steps to augment the international community's knowledge base in order to facilitate adequate environmental protection from mining. These steps include standardizing data and data collection methods in order to develop robust databases to facilitate decision-making. On the development of appropriate technologies, recent advances in submersible technologies suggest that operating depths of over 7,000 metres will soon be surpassed. The number of requests to the Commission on the Outer Limits of the Continental Shelf to demarcate the limits of many coastal States bodes well for those States that wish to exploit the mineral resources in this geographic area. It is becoming clear that exploitation of marine mineral resources is increasingly likely and with this increase in activity, the potential impacts on the marine environment need to be addressed, particularly as concerns environmental impact assessments. The Authority will begin work on an exploitation

code next year and this code is expected to include the requirement for environmental impact assessment, which is why we are holding this meeting.

As you will have seen from the agenda, the aims of this workshop are:

- To raise awareness of the nature of the mineral resources in the seabed beyond the limits of national jurisdiction ("the Area"), and on the outer continental shelf, and the measures taken by the International Seabed Authority with regard to the protection of the marine environment from the harmful effects of deep seabed mining and the applicability of such measures to the development of marine minerals within national jurisdiction.

- To formulate preliminary recommendations for environmental impact assessments of seabed mining in areas within and beyond national jurisdiction.

I want to thank you for participating in this workshop and for those making presentations, to acknowledge with appreciation the readiness with which you agreed to make them and to contribute to the proceedings. I look forward to productive discussions during the next few days and I will now pass the microphone to Adam Cook, the Authority's scientific affairs officer responsible for marine biology, who with Akuila Tawake of SPC are the facilitators for the workshop and who will provide more information on the structure of the workshop and what the Authority would like to achieve from it.

Presentations at the Workshop

Session 1: Marine mineral resources

Marine mineral resources of the Asia-Pacific region within and beyond national jurisdiction. *Jim Hein, United States Geological Survey (USGS)*

Seafloor massive sulphide (SMS) potential within and beyond national jurisdiction in the Asia-Pacific region. *Ray Binns, The Commonwealth Scientific and Industrial Research Organisation (CSIRO)*

Global marine potential for rare earth elements (REEs) and recent developments. *Jim Hein, United States Geological Survey (USGS)*

Session 2: The legal regime for the development of marine mineral resources

The International Seabed Authority: Structure and functions. *Nii Allotey Odunton, ISA*

The legal regime for the development of the mineral resources of the Area. *Michael Lodge, ISA*

The legal regime for the development of marine mineral resources within national jurisdiction. *Hannah Lily, SPC SOPAC Division*

Session 3: Environmental regulation

The potential environmental impact of seabed mining. *Charles Morgan, Planning Solutions, Inc.*

International standards for the protection of the marine environment. *Robin Warner, The Australian National Centre for Ocean Resources & Security, University of Wollongong*

Session 4: Protection of the marine environment in the Area

What baseline and monitoring data are needed for environmental protection from marine mining in the Area? *Chuck Fisher, Pennsylvania State University*

Status of technology relevant to the protection of the marine environment. *Robert Heydon, Nauru Ocean Resources Inc.*

Marine conservation perspectives and concerns for deep sea mining. *Jan Steffen, International Union for Conservation of Nature (IUCN)*

Session 5: ISA initiatives for environmental protection

The environmental work of the International Seabed Authority, including the status of exploration contractors' work in the Clarion-Clipperton Zone. *Adam Cook, ISA*

Standardization of environmental data. *Malcolm Clark, the National Institute of Water and Atmospheric Research (NIWA)*

Session 6: Regional initiatives and case studies

SPC-EU Deep Sea Minerals Project. *Akuila Tawake, SPC SOPAC Division*

Outcomes of the Western South Pacific Regional Workshop to Facilitate the Description of Ecologically or Biologically Significant Marine Areas (EBSAs). *Nic Bax, University of Tasmania*

Case study: Nautilus Minerals Inc. Solwara 1 Project. *Samantha Smith, Nautilus Minerals Inc.*

Session 7: National case studies

Tonga. *Paula Taumoepeau, Nautilus Minerals Tonga and Kate McPherson, Ministry of Environment and Climate Change, Tonga*

Cook Islands. *Paul Lynch, Adviser to the Minister for Marine Resources and Minerals and Seabed Mining Taskforce, Cook Islands*

Papua New Guinea. *Lyndah Brown-Kola, Mineral Resources Authority, Papua New Guinea*

Fiji. *Malakai Finau, Ministry of Lands and Minerals Resources, Fiji*

Nauru. *Bryan Starr, Ministry of Commerce, Industry and Environment, Nauru*

Kiribati. *Tearinaki Tanielu, Ministry of Fisheries and Marine Resources Development, Kiribati*

Japan. *Tetsuhiko Toyohara, Japan Oil, Gas and Metals National Corporation (JOGMEC), Japan*

All presentations and video recordings of their delivery are available at
http://www.isa.org.jm/en/scientific/workshops/2011

Introduction

The Authority is the organization through which States parties to the 1982 United Nations Convention on the Law of the Sea (the "Convention" or "UNCLOS"), in accordance with Part XI of the Convention, organize and control activities in the Area, particularly with a view to administering the resources of the Area. This is to be done in accordance with the regime for deep seabed mining established in Part XI and other related provisions of the Convention and in the Agreement relating to the Implementation of Part XI of the United Nations Convention on the Law of the Sea of 10 December 1982 (the "1994 Agreement") adopted by the General Assembly of the United Nations under the terms of its resolution 48/263 of 28 July 1994.

The Authority has a broad role to play in relation to the protection and preservation of the marine environment. Under articles 143 and 145 of the Convention the Authority has a general responsibility to promote and encourage the conduct of marine scientific research in the Area. It also has a duty to ensure effective protection of the marine environment from harmful effects which may arise from mining-related activities in the Area.

The duties of the Authority under the Convention with respect to the marine environment were given added emphasis in the 1994 Agreement, which, inter alia, requires the Authority to give priority to the adoption of rules, regulations and procedures incorporating applicable standards for the protection and preservation of the marine environment[1] and requires that an application for approval of a plan of work for exploration is accompanied by an assessment of the potential environmental impacts of the proposed exploration activities and a description of a programme for oceanographic and baseline environmental studies.[2] Annex III to the Convention, which sets out the basic conditions of prospecting, exploration and exploitation, also requires the Authority to adopt rules, regulations and procedures on mining standards and practices, including those relating to the protection of the marine environment.[3]

In addition to those provisions, article 165, paragraph 2, of the Convention requires the Legal and Technical Commission (LTC) to inter alia: make recommendations to the Council on the protection of the marine environment; take into account assessments of environmental implications when formulating rules, regulations and procedures referred to in article 162, paragraph 2 (o), of the Convention; and make recommendations to the Council regarding the establishment of a monitoring programme.

These various provisions of the Convention and the Agreement have been given substance through Regulations progressively issued by the Authority governing activities in relation to specific mineral resources. The first set of Regulations, adopted in 2000, dealt with polymetallic nodules. The second set of Regulations, adopted in 2010, govern prospecting and exploration for polymetallic sulphides. It is anticipated that Regulations for prospecting and exploration for cobalt-rich ferromanganese crusts will be adopted in 2012.

A remotely operated vehicle ROV) being deployed to study the seafloor. © Nautilus Minerals

[1]   1994 Agreement, annex, Section 1, paragraph 5(g).
[2]   1994 Agreement, annex, Section 1, paragraph 7.
[3]   Annex III, article 17, paragraph (1)(b)(xii).

The regulatory regime

The scheme set out in the Regulations is broadly as follows. Firstly, as required by article 145 of the Convention, the Authority is under a duty to establish and keep under review environmental rules, regulations and procedures to ensure effective protection for the marine environment from harmful effects which may arise from activities in the Area.[4] To this end, Regulation 1(5) provides that the Regulations may be supplemented by further rules, regulations and procedures, in particular on the protection and preservation of the marine environment. Secondly, the Authority and sponsoring States are required to apply a precautionary approach, as reflected in Principle 15 of the Rio Declaration, to activities in the Area.[5] The LTC is to make recommendations to the Council on the implementation of this requirement. Thirdly, the Regulations impose a duty on each contractor to "take necessary measures to prevent, reduce and control pollution and other hazards to the marine environment arising from its activities in the Area as far as reasonably possible using the best technology available to it."

To give practical effect to these broad principles, the Regulations contain an important provision which enables the LTC to issue from time to time, recommendations of a technical or administrative nature for the guidance of contractors, to assist them in the implementation of the rules, regulations and procedures. Contractors with the Authority are required to observe any such recommendations as far as reasonably practicable.

A key factor for the Authority is that, although a significant amount of basic and applied research has been carried out or is still in progress, it is broadly accepted that the current level of knowledge and understanding of deep-sea ecology does not make it possible to issue any conclusive risk assessment of the effects of large-scale commercial seabed mining. In order to be able in future to manage the impact of mineral development in the Area in such a way as to prevent harmful effects to the marine environment, it is essential for the Authority to have better knowledge of the state and vulnerability of the marine environment in mineral-bearing provinces. This includes knowledge of baseline conditions in these areas, the natural variability of these baseline conditions and the relationship with impacts related to mining.

For this reason, the Regulations emphasize the progressive nature of exploration and mining activities. Contractors are required to collect baseline data as an integral part of their exploration programmes and provide these data to the Authority in standardized formats. The characteristics of the data to be collected are informed by the international workshops convened by the Authority, which include not only representatives of contractors, but also internationally-recognized scientific experts. These workshops also inform the work of the LTC.

In 2001, the LTC issued a series of Recommendations for the guidance of contractors for the assessment of the possible environmental impacts arising from exploration for polymetallic nodules in the Area. These were revised in 2010 (ISBA/16/LTC/7). These Recommendations, which were based on proposals made at the Authority's first environmental workshop held in China in 1998 and subsequent workshops, list the baseline data that should be collected by contractors and identify the activities that will require environmental impact assessment. This includes test, or "pilot" mining, which would be assessed and evaluated for its impact on the marine environment prior to the issue of a permit for large-scale commercial mining. The primary source of baseline information for such an assessment will be the data that have been progressively collected by contractors over many years of exploration activity.

Neither the Regulations, nor the Recommendations for Guidance, specify the scope and format of an environmental impact assessment.

---

4   Regulation 31(1). See also the 1982 Convention, article 165, paragraphs (2)(e), (f) and (h), Annex III, article 17, paragraph 1(b)(xii) and 17, paragraph 2(f); 1994 Agreement, annex, Section 1, paragraph 5(g).

5   Principle 15 of the Rio Declaration states as follows: 'In order to protect the environment, the precautionary approach shall be widely applied by States according to their capabilities. Where there are threats of serious or irreversible damage, lack of full scientific certainty shall not be used as a reason for postponing cost-effective measures to prevent environmental degradation'. U.N. Doc. A/CONF./151/26 (Vol.1). Available at: http://www.un.org/documents/ga/conf151/aconf15126-1annex1.htm.

The Fiji workshop

The Fiji workshop was convened to follow up on the increasing interest in and associated concerns about the potential impacts of deep sea minerals exploration and mining and how responsible authorities will regulate this emerging economic development opportunity in a sustainable manner, both within national jurisdiction and in the Area. The workshop was attended by 79 participants from 18 countries, and was supported by the secretariat of the International Seabed Authority and the SPC. The full list of participants can be found in the Annex to this document.

Working group discussions during the 2011 workshop

The workshop was organized to raise awareness of the nature of the mineral resources found in the seabed beyond the limits of national jurisdiction ("the Area") and on the outer continental shelf, and of the measures taken by the International Seabed Authority with respect to the protection of the marine environment from the harmful effects of deep seabed mining and the applicability of such measures to the development of marine minerals within national jurisdiction. The outputs from the workshop included a draft template for an environmental impact assessment of seabed mining; an outline of the legislative and regulatory provisions that should form the basis of environmental management of deep seabed mining; and the identification of capacity-building needs and methods by which these needs could be

addressed. The objective of the present report is to disseminate the outcomes of the discussions at the workshop, the full proceedings of the workshop will be published in due course.

The workshop began with a series of presentations which are archived on the Authority's website (http://www.isa.org.jm/en/scientific/ workshops/2011). Participants then split into three working groups to address specific questions that had been highlighted as priority areas.

The first working group was tasked with preparing an EIA template that could be used in the first instance by exploration contractors when carrying out activities requiring an EIA, whilst ensuring that the template was broad enough so that it would be applicable to exploitation. The template was also designed to provide assistance to developing States when preparing their own regulatory regimes for seabed activities within national jurisdiction, including, but not restricted to, seabed mineral exploration and exploitation. Whilst not conclusive, it is designed to stand as a template that can be adapted as appropriate depending on the situation. The template can be found later in this document.

The second working group addressed the legislative and regulatory provisions that should form the basis of environmental management of deep seabed mining activities, in areas within and beyond international jurisdiction. Whilst the international legislative regime for mineral exploration beyond national jurisdiction is well established through the activities of the Authority, work is only just beginning on the development of regulations addressing exploitation-related activities. Nor have there been to date any precedents for national-level legislation to govern the relationship between sponsoring States and sponsored Contractors in the Area – a requirement of sponsoring States that was highlighted by the Advisory Opinion issued in February 2011 by the Seabed Disputes Chamber of the International Tribunal for the Law of the Sea (ITLOS). In addition, in recent times there has been increased interest in marine mineral exploitation within the national jurisdiction of various countries, particularly among PICs who had expressed a need to develop national regulatory frameworks for this purpose. The working group decided that it was not appropriate to draft a detailed legislative model for the regulation of deep seabed mining but that it would be more helpful to identify key legislation and international obligations that should be considered by States when discussing both the development of the exploitation code for minerals beyond national jurisdiction and also their national legislation.

The third working group focused on identifying the capacity-building needs associated with seabed mining, particularly those related to environmental impact assessment. The group noted that the current level of technical, human and financial capacity impinged upon the ability of developing countries to engage in seabed mining and also to evaluate the potential impact of such activities, both within national jurisdiction and in the Area. The working group identified a series of activities that could help to address the capacity-building requirements of developing States.

This publication is intended to serve to act as a catalyst to future discussions of environmental impact assessment of seabed mining. It is expected that the ideas contained within the working group reports will evolve into a series of programmes which will ensure that seabed mining progresses in an environmentally sound manner and also that developing States can fully engage in the commercial, legislative and environmental activities associated with seabed mining in areas within and beyond national jurisdiction.

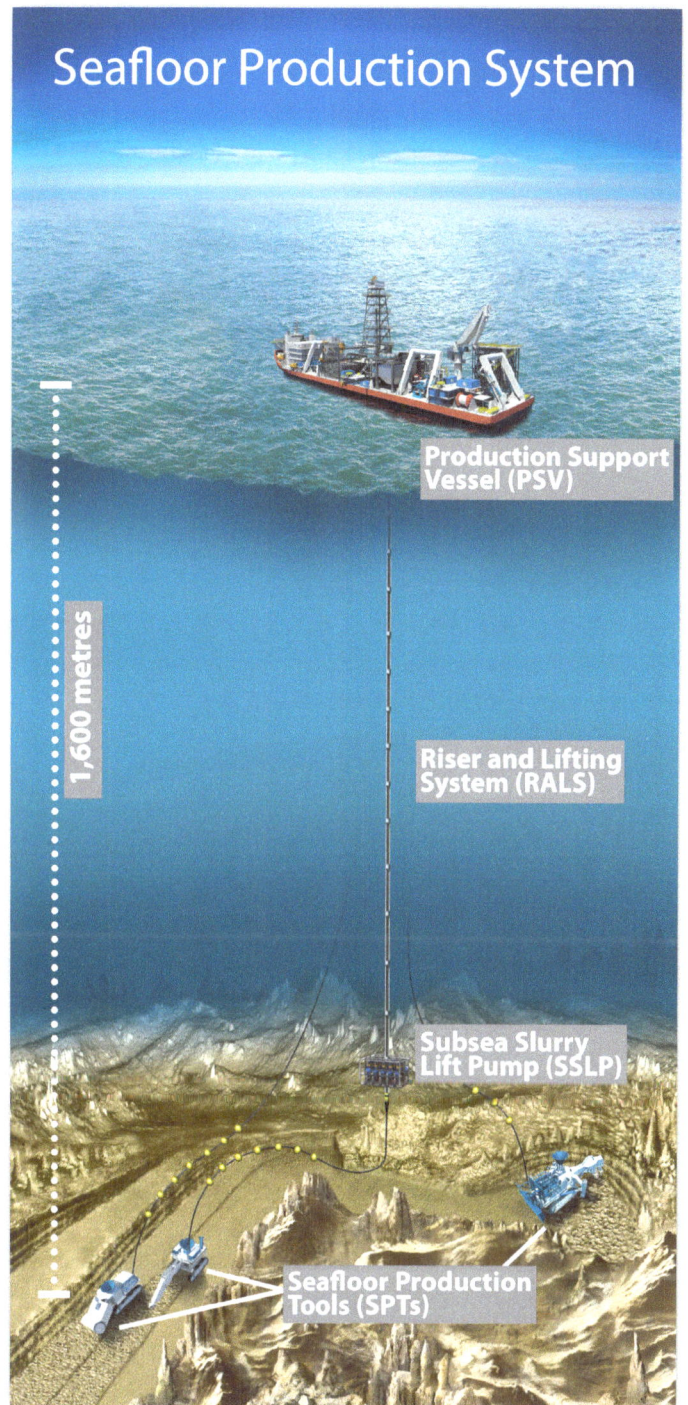

Seafloor Production System

1,600 metres

Production Support Vessel (PSV)

Riser and Lifting System (RALS)

Subsea Slurry Lift Pump (SSLP)

Seafloor Production Tools (SPTs)

An example of a commercial seabed mining system. © Nautilus minerals

Environmental Impact Assessment

Introduction

Under UNCLOS, States Parties have a general obligation to protect and preserve the marine environment. This obligation encompasses responsibilities to prevent, reduce and control the potential effects of activities which may cause substantial pollution of, or significant and harmful changes to, the marine environment. In the deep seabed beyond national jurisdiction, the Authority, on behalf of the States Parties to UNCLOS, is responsible for administering the mineral resources of the Area, including prospecting, exploration, and exploitation activities for these resources. As part of its responsibility, the Authority is charged with taking the necessary measures to ensure effective protection for the marine environment from harmful effects which may arise from such activities.

As part of the progression of mining operations from exploration to exploitation, there is a strong need for detailed environmental assessment, and the development of a formal Environmental Impact Assessment (EIA) process by the Authority. At the International Workshop on Environmental Management Needs for Exploration and Exploitation of Deep Sea Minerals, held in Nadi, Fiji, a working group was convened to formulate a provisional template for guiding the format of an EIA by companies wishing to apply for exploration licences.

The template that has been developed represents a generalized framework, which is targeted at the requirements of the Authority for the Area, but is also intended to be applicable for deep sea mining (DSM) inside EEZs. The template is designed with the three main types of DSM in mind: polymetallic nodules, seafloor massive sulphides and cobalt-rich ferromanganese crusts. Furthermore, several EIA sections provide the opportunity to utilize the results of baseline data collection and test-mining activities during the preceding exploratory phases. The template is not designed to be prescriptive, but to enable sufficient flexibility to be suitable for a wide range of situations and information levels. Brief notes are included on the required content of

sections and subsections, but the working group acknowledged there was further work to be done in expanding guidelines on completion of the EIA.

The information that follows is intended to assist and guide prospective developers planning to carry out mineral exploitation activities. It should be noted that some sections would be more relevant to activities in areas within national jurisdiction, rather than to activities in the Area.

The developer must submit an Environmental Impact Statement (EIS) that provides full documentation of all environmental and social issues and committing to the application of relevant mitigation measures in relation to the development activity. The EIS should substantially comply with this Technical Guidance Document. It should be noted that the EIA process and the EIS are key inputs, together with comments received from referral bodies and other stakeholders, that will be used by the Authority to assess whether or not a proposal is recommended for approval.

The recommended format for the EIS is outlined below. It is intended to provide the Authority and other stakeholders with unambiguous documentation of potential environmental impacts on which the Authority can base its assessment and any subsequent approval that may be granted.

Human activity on seamounts can be very damaging if not suitably regulated. © National Institute of Water & Atmospheric Research Ltd.

Content of the Environmental Impact Statement

The applicant should provide detailed responses to all areas below that are relevant to the development proposal.

Executive summary

One of the main objectives of this section is to provide an explanation of the project for non-technical readers. Information provided in the executive summary should briefly describe:

    A.   the proposed development activity and its objectives;

    B.   anticipated bio-physical and socio-economic impacts (direct/indirect, reversible/ irreversible) of the activity;

    C.   details of remedial actions that are proposed;

    D.   the benefits to be derived from the project;

    E.   details of the consultation programme undertaken by the applicant, including degree of public interest; and

    F.   end-use plans for the development activity.

The summary should not be more than 15 pages in length and in English. Appendices should be attached, as appropriate, to the EIS in order to provide complete information on the development proposal.

Introduction

Background

This section should briefly summarize the project being proposed.

Project history

This section should briefly summarize the work undertaken up to the date to the EIS was finalized and ready to be submitted. This should include a brief description of the deposit discovery and the exploration and test mining activities conducted to date.

Project proponent

This section should summarize the credentials of the Contractor proposing the development, including major shareholders, other tenements owned or applied for, and their jurisdictions, etc.

Purpose of and justification for the development

The purpose of this section is to ensure that only development activities that are in line with the Authority's goals and objectives are considered for approval. This section should provide information on the viability of the proposed development activity. These details should include, but not limited to, the following:

    A. the capital cost associated with the development;

    B. the proponent's technological expertise and resources;

    C. results of any feasibility investigations that have been carried out;

    D. the extent of landowner and/or resource owner support, including a copy of the formal written approval of their consent;

    E. the anticipated lifespan and development phases of the project.

This Report

    Statutory context

    EIS scope

    Report structure

Policy, legal and administrative framework

This section should provide information on relevant legislation, agreements or policies that are applicable to the proposed mining operation. It is separated into four sections, each covering a different aspect of the legal framework.

Applicable mining and environmental legislation, policy and agreements

The applicant should note any legislation, regulation or guidelines that apply to the management, or regulation of mining, or the environment in the Area, or any other relevant (existing or proposed) jurisdiction. This should include a note on how the proposed operation will comply with these requirements.

Other legislation, policy and regulations

Description of any other legislation, policy or regulations that do not apply specifically to mining or environment, but may be relevant to the proposal (e.g. shipping regulations, offshore mining certificates, and potentially many more inside jurisdictional boundaries).

Relevant international agreements

This subsection describes other more general international agreements that could be applicable to the operation, such as UNCLOS, CBD regulations and UNGA resolutions.

Environmental
Other

International standards, principles and guidelines

Any other non-legal standards or guidelines that may apply to best practice in the operation, e.g. Equator Principles.

Stakeholder consultation

This section describes any consultation(s) that may have taken place with interested parties and stakeholders with an interest in the DSM application in the period leading up to the application.

Relevant jurisdiction consultation requirements

This outlines any international or jurisdictional consultation obligations.

Stakeholders

List any relevant stakeholders or other interested parties that have been consulted.

Public consultation and disclosure programme

Description of the goals and consultation workshops/meetings that have occurred prior to the preparation of the report.

Goals
Consultation methods
Scientific workshops
Cultural heritage

Consultation outcomes

Continuing consultation

What further consultation with stakeholders is needed?

Description of the proposed development

All relevant details on the proposed development activity required under this section should be provided where applicable to the proposal. Details to be provided under this section may include the headings listed below.

Project area definition

Location

This section should include detailed location maps (drawn to scale), site layout, etc.

Associated activities

This section should include a description of any supporting activities and infrastructure required (e.g. ports, barges, transportation corridors, crew transfers, etc.)

Project components

This section should provide background information to the proposal, technologies to be employed, etc. For polymetallic nodule exploitation, Contractors should refer to Section IV C of the Recommendations for the guidance of contractors for the assessment of the possible environmental impacts arising from exploration for polymetallic nodules in the Area (ISBA/16/LTC/7). This section should include information on methods of exploitation site selection including alternatives investigated, relevant diagrams and drawings.

Mining

Transport/materials handling

On-site processing

Alternatives considered and rejected from analysis

Mining

Transport/materials handling

On-site processing

Mineral resource

This section should include the type of resource proposed for extraction (e.g. nodules, polymetallic sulphides, cobalt-rich crusts or other mineral), the type of commodity, the grade and volume. Estimates of inferred and indicated resource should be provided.

Offshore mining and support equipment

This section should include descriptions of the offshore mining and support equipment (including vessels) required to carry out the activity.

Mining

Mine plan

General mining sequence

Hazardous materials management

Description of hazardous materials

Transportation

Storage, handling and disposal

Workforce

Workforce description

Employment policy

Capacity-building objectives and commitments

Construction and operating standards

This section should outline the design codes to which the equipment will be built, as well as the health and safety standards that will be applied.

Design codes

Health and safety

Commissioning

Decommissioning and closure

Offshore infrastructure

Onshore facilities

Development timetable (Detailed schedule)

Description of the overall timetable, from implementation of the mining programme through to decommissioning and closure of operations. This should include the major phases of the operation, as well as the milestone dates on which relevant tasks are expected to be completed. Information on the development timetable provided under this section should clearly communicate the different phases in the development proposal. For reasons of clarity, a Flow chart, Gantt or PERT chart should be used where appropriate. Information provided in this section should include, but not be limited to, the following:

A. *The funding arrangement for proposed activity or if availability of funds is subject to this or other approvals being granted;*

B. *Pre-construction activities;*

C. *Construction schedule, staging, etc.;*

D. *Commissioning and operational schedules;*

E. *Infrastructure development schedule; and*

F. *Closure schedule.*

Description of the existing offshore environment

In this section, the applicant is to give a detailed account of knowledge of the environmental conditions at the site. It provides the baseline description of geological, oceanographic and biological conditions against which impacts will be measured and assessed.

Regional overview

Provide a general description of the environmental conditions in the broad region of the site, including major oceanographic, geological and biological setting.

Studies completed

Description of any prior research/exploration activities which could provide relevant information for this EIA and future activities. These should be detailed in the appendices, and submission of the environmental reference baseline data collected for the Authority, as outlined in exploration licence conditions; Section III of the "Recommendations for the guidance of contractors for the assessment of the possible environmental impacts arising from exploration for polymetallic nodules in the Area" (IBSA/16/LTC/7) should accompany this EIS.

Special considerations for site

Description of any notable characteristics of the site, whether geological, oceanographic or biological, such as hydrothermal venting, seamounts, high-surface productivity, eddies and endemic fauna.

Meteorology and air quality

Geological setting

Description of the general geological landscape and topographic features of the site.

Physical oceanographic setting

Description of oceanographic aspects such as currents, sedimentation rates.

Water quality

Description of water mass characteristics at the site at various depths, including nutrients, particle loads, temperature and dissolved gas profiles, etc.

Sediment characteristics

Description of substrate composition with special reference to sediment composition, pore water profiles, and grain size.

Biological environment

This section is divided by depth regime into a description of the various biological components and communities that are present in or utilize the water column and seabed in the region of the site.

Pelagic

From the surface down to 200m. This includes plankton, surface/near surface fish, such as tunas, but also utilization by seabirds and marine mammals.

Midwater

Open water from a depth of 200m down to the seafloor. This includes zooplankton, mesopelagic and bathypelagic fishes and deep-diving mammals.

Benthic

Benthic invertebrate communities, including infauna and demersal fish. This should include considerations of species richness, biodiversity, faunal densities and community structures.

Natural hazards

Description of volcanism, seismic activity, etc.

Noise

Description of ambient noise if any, influence of ongoing exploration and maritime activity.

Description of the existing onshore environment

Description of the conditions of any onshore processing operation, as well as any relevant environmental information on transit lanes/areas.

Socio-economic environment
If the project area occurs within an area used by fisheries, then this needs to be described here.

Existing resource utilization

Fisheries

Marine traffic
This section describes the non-project-related marine traffic occurring within the project area.

Other
This section will deal with other uses of the project area that are not related to fisheries or marine traffic (e.g. telecommunications cables, other mineral exploitation projects, etc.).

Cultural/historical resources
This section will deal with items of cultural/historical significance that occur within the project area (e.g. shipwrecks).

Socio-economic and socio-cultural issues
Issues that may arise within and outside of the project area should be identified, including whether this is a direct or indirect outcome of the physical, biological or socio-economic effects of the proposed development activity.

Onshore socio-economic environment
It is envisaged that this section will only be applicable to projects located within EEZs.

Environmental impacts, mitigation and management measures
In this section, the applicant is to provide a detailed description and evaluation of potential impacts of the mining operation to environmental components identified previously. The format should be consistent between and within sections, so for each component a description would be included of:

  A. the nature and extent of any impact;

  B. measures that will be taken to avoid, mitigate or minimize such impact; and

  C. what unavoidable impacts will remain.

It is expected that some repetition will occur between sections, notably where an impact of the mining operation will affect several components of the environment at the site.

Description of potential impact categories
This section is an overview and description of general impact categories caused by the mining operation. This is not expected to be detailed, but introduce the major types of effect, such as habitat removal, crushing of animals, creation of sediment plumes, noise, light etc. A description should be included of any lessons learnt from activities during the exploratory phase of the programme (e.g. test mining trials).

Results of test mining operations

Description of the test mining activity

Location and scale of operation

Non-proprietary description of equipment used

Non-proprietary description of ore recovered

Description of impact assessment activities
Sampling equipment, sample types, locations, replication, measurements, monitoring, etc.

Results of impact assessment activities
Reference paragraphs 17 and 18 of the "Recommendations for the guidance of contractors for the assessment of the possible environmental impacts arising from exploration for polymetallic nodules in the Area" (ISBA/16/LTC/7) and place full results in an appendix.

Air quality
Description of any effect on the air quality from the surface or subsurface operations.

Impacts and issues to be addressed

Environmental management measures

Residual impacts

Geological setting
Description of impacts the mining may have on the topography of the site or geological/geophysical composition.

Impacts and issues to be addressed

Environmental management measures

Residual impacts

Physical oceanographic setting
Description of effects on current speed/direction, sedimentation rates, etc.

Impacts and issues to be addressed

Environmental management measures

Residual impacts

Water quality
Description of effects such as sediment plume generation and clarity of water, particulate loading, water temperature, dissolved gas and nutrient levels etc., in all levels of the water column.

Impacts and issues to be addressed

Environmental management measures

Residual impacts

Sediment characteristics
e.g. changes in the sediment composition, grain size, density, pore water profiles.

Impacts and issues to be addressed

Environmental management measures

Residual impacts

Biological communities

Description of the effects on individuals, communities, populations and meta-populations from the proposed activity.

Pelagic

Includes plankton, surface/near-surface fish, such as tunas, but also seabirds and marine mammals.

Impacts and issues to be addressed

Environmental management measures

Residual impacts

Midwater

Includes zooplankton, mesopelagic and bathypelagic fishes and deep-diving mammals.

Impacts and issues to be addressed

Environmental management measures

Residual impacts

Benthic

e.g. Benthic epifaunal and infaunal invertebrate communities and demersal fish.

Impacts and issues to be addressed

Environmental management measures

Residual impacts

Natural hazards

e.g. Volcanic eruptions, seismic activity, sea floor instability and tsunami.

Impacts and issues to be addressed

Environmental management measures

Residual impacts

Noise

Noise above existing levels

Impacts and issues to be addressed

Environmental management measures

Residual impacts

Greenhouse gas emissions and climate change

Effects of surface/subsurface activities on GHG emissions and any activity that may affect water acidity.

Estimated GHG emissions

GHG emissions assessment

Maritime safety and interactions with shipping

Issues to be addressed

Mitigation and management measures

Project safety

Interaction with other vessels

Residual impacts

Biosecurity
e.g. ballast water issues and ship movement into the area and out for servicing / processing.

Issues to be addressed

Mitigation and management measures

Residual impacts

Waste management
Vessel waste management, with reference to compliance with relevant conventions, legislation or principles, methods of cleaner production and energy balance.

Impacts and issues to be addressed

Mitigation and management measures

Residual impacts

Cumulative impacts
Here the proposer should consider the nature and extent of any interactions between various impacts, where they may have cumulative effects.

Proposed operations impacts
Cumulative within the scope of the mining proposed herein.

Regional operation impacts
Cumulative between activities where known in the region.

On- and nearshore environment
Where appropriate this should contain a description of general issues related to transit from/to the site and port operation, etc. This subsection is to be developed in as much detail as appropriate, with emphasis on the particular circumstances of the mining operation and processing location.

Issues to be addressed

Mitigation and management measures

Residual impacts

Socio-economic impacts
In this section, the applicant is to provide a description and evaluation of potential impacts of the mining operation to previously identified socio-economic components. The format is consistent between sections.

Existing resource utilization

Fisheries

Issues

Mitigation and management

Residual impacts

Marine traffic

Issues

Mitigation and management

Residual impacts

Other (e.g. telecommunications)

Issues

Mitigation and management

Residual impacts

Cultural/Historical resources (e.g. shipwrecks, IUCN natural world heritage sites)

Issues

Mitigation and management

Residual impacts

Socio-economic and socio-cultural issues

This section will provide a description of elements of economic benefit or impact, community development, industry diversity and skills development, migration and community conflicts.

Issues to be addressed

These include aspects, such as supply chain, utilities, access to water, fuel, and impact to local communities in terms of access to supplies.

Mitigation and management measures

e.g. project benefits, consultation efforts, etc.

Residual impacts

Accidental Events and Natural Hazards

Environmentally hazardous discharges resulting from accidental and extreme natural events are fundamentally different from normal operational discharges of wastes and waste waters. This section should outline the possibility/probability of accidental events occurring, the impact they may have, the measures taken to prevent or respond to such an event, and the residual impact should an event occur.

Extreme weather

Issues to be addressed

Mitigation and management measures

Residual impacts

Natural hazards

e.g. volcanic eruption, seismic events, landslides and soil erosion.

Issues to be addressed

Mitigation and management measures

Residual impacts

Accidental events

e.g Hazardous material leakage or spillage, fire and explosion, collisions, including potential loss of equipment.

Issues to be addressed

Mitigation and management measures

Residual impacts

Environmental management, monitoring and reporting

Sufficient information should be provided to enable the Authority to anticipate possible environmental management, monitoring and reporting requirements for an environment permit. Information listed should reflect the proponent's environmental policy (Environment Management System) and the translation of that policy to meet the requirements under this section and previous sections during different stages in the project life, i.e. from operations to decommissioning and closure. Information detailed in this section should include, but not be limited to, the headings below.

Organizational structure and responsibilities

This section should show how the Contractor's environmental team fits into its overall organizational structure. Responsibilities of key personnel should be outlined.

Environmental Management System (EMS)

It is understood that a full EMS may or may not exist at the EIS submission stage. This section should outline the standards that will be considered and/or aligned with in developing the EMS for the project.

Environmental Management Plan (EMP)

An EMP will be submitted as a separate document for the Authority's approval prior to exploitation operations commencing. This section should provide an overview of what an EMP would entail. This section shall include, as a minimum, the following headings.

Mitigation and management

This section should summarize the actions and commitments that have arisen from the impact minimization and mitigation strategies.

Monitoring plan

This section should summarize the monitoring plan approach and programme. For development proposals associated with nodule exploitation, Contractors should take into account sections IV(D) and IV(E) of the "Recommendations for the guidance of contractors for the assessment of the possible environmental impacts arising from exploration for polymetallic nodules in the Area (ISBA/16/LTC/7).

Approach

Programme

This section should provide an overview of the envisaged monitoring programme (it is noted further detail will be provided in the EMP).

Closure plan

It is expected that a closure plan will be submitted as a separate document for the Authority's approval. However, this section should provide an overview of what the closure plan will entail, including decommissioning, continued monitoring and rehabilitation measures, if applicable.

> **Reporting**
>
> > **Monitoring**
> > *Results of monitoring studies should be reported to the Authority.*
> >
> > **Incident reporting**
> > *Any incidents must be reported.*
>
> **Study team**
> *This section should outline the people involved in carrying out the Environmental Impact Assessment studies and in writing the environmental impact statement. If independent scientists or other experts were involved in any of the work, they should be listed under "EIS Specialist Sub consultants".*
>
> > **Proponent**
> >
> > **Lead environmental consultant(s)**
> >
> > **EIS specialist sub-consultants**
>
> **References**
> *This section should provide details of reference materials used in sourcing information and/or data used in the Environmental Impact Statement.*
>
> **Glossary and abbreviations**
>
> **Annex**
> *All supporting studies should be attached in an annex.*

Contractors should ensure all non-proprietary environmental data from supporting studies, exploration and test mining has been provided to The Authority in electronic format, as specified by the Authority, prior to submitting the EIS for review by the Authority.

Confidential information: Details of classified information relating to a manufacturing or industrial process or trade secret used in carrying on or operating any particular undertaking or equipment or information of a business or financial nature in relation to the proposed activity should be clearly defined. Such information would be classified as "confidential information" and excluded from the EIS before the document is made available for public review.

Fauna on an undisturbed hydrothermal vent
© National Science Foundation Ridge 2000 Program and Charles Fisher, Penn State University

Legal Issues

Introduction

The Working Group on Legal Issues was established to identify the legislative and regulatory provisions for the environmental management of deep seabed mining activities in areas within and beyond international jurisdiction.

Accordingly, the Working Group did not consider wider legislative and regulatory issues, such the payment of royalties or taxes which fell outside the scope of workshop. Furthermore, the Working Group decided not to draft a detailed legislative model for regulation of deep seabed mining because the first step in preparing legislative instructions is to identify key policies that need to be reflected in the legislation.

The Working Group decided to focus on those parts of a national legislative template that dealt with:

- International obligations;
- The powers, duties and functions of the administering authority; and
- Permit/licence requirements and environmental impact assessment.

Preliminary issues

Deep seabed minerals legislation ("the Act") is required to be implemented by States sponsoring or licensing deep sea mining (DSM) activities. This legislation could either be integrated into existing environmental legislation or could be issued as stand-alone legislation. The principle of integrated management suggests that fewer legislative instruments facilitate efficient and timely decision-making.

The proposed Act should contain high-level statements on EIA obligations and other international law obligations. The Working Group considered that the best approach would be for such provisions to form a preliminary 'purpose and principles' part of the Act, against which decision-making under the Act would be considered. This is consistent with a purpose-based approach to legislative drafting.

The Working Group acknowledged that international environmental law obligations are the same in areas within and beyond national jurisdiction, and should be reflected as such in national legislation that addresses activities in one or the other of these jurisdictions. However, differences in relation to the administration of DSM in the areas beyond national jurisdiction arise due to the additional role of the Authority and the geographical remoteness of these activities from areas under national control. This should be reflected in the legislation, e.g. there may be differences arising in relation to sponsorship requirements, and timing and components of EIA. The Authority's Mining Code could serve as a useful drafting tool for such legislation.

Provisions for consideration of transboundary impacts should be included in the legislation, e.g. a requirement for a State responsible for an impact to provide timely information to another State which may be affected, and an opportunity for both States to participate in environmental decision-making procedures.

An essential prerequisite for good administration and a clear regulatory framework for investments, is for countries to delineate maritime boundaries in accordance with UNCLOS, including outer continental shelf delimitations and maritime boundaries with adjacent countries. One potential approach to consider in cases of maritime boundary disputes are joint development zones for offshore mining.

International obligations

- The Working Group identified the following obligations under international law as overarching principles that should be incorporated in any statutory framework for offshore mining: Duty to protect and preserve marine environment (Article 192, UNCLOS);

- Precautionary approach (Principle 15 of Rio Declaration; ITLOS Advisory Opinion; ISA Mining Code);

- Duty to prevent, reduce and control pollution from seabed activities (Article 208, UNCLOS);

- Best environmental practice (ISA Mining Code, ITLOS Advisory Opinion);

- Duty to prevent transboundary harm (Part XII, UNCLOS; ITLOS Advisory Opinion: Rio Declaration);

- Duty to conserve biodiversity (Article 3, CBD);

- Prior EIA of activities likely to cause significant harm (Article 206, UNCLOS);

- Ongoing monitoring of environmental impacts (Article 204, UNCLOS);

- Sustainable development and integrated management (widely implemented in existing domestic legislation of countries within the region, e.g. Fiji, Cook Islands, New Zealand and Australia).

The following principles might also be included:

- 'Polluter pays' principle (Rio Declaration);

- Regional cooperation/integration in monitoring, processing and capacity-building (Articles 276-277, UNCLOS);

- Identifying mechanisms of capacity building (Part XI, UNCLOS);

- Accountability and transparency (Aarhus Convention).

The Working Group agreed that powers, duties and functions under the Act should be consistent with UNCLOS. An example of wholesale incorporation into domestic legislation was noted in New Zealand's EEZ and Continental Shelf (Environmental Effects) Bill; clause 11 of this Bill states that: "This Act must be interpreted, and all persons performing functions and duties or exercising powers under it must act, consistently with New Zealand's international obligations under the LOSC."

An example of the localized impact created by a nodule mining collecting system. © IFREMER

Administering authority –
Powers, duties and functions

Regulating body

The Working Group identified the need for a specialized body to regulate, on behalf of a State, operators performing deep seabed mining activities within that State's control or jurisdiction. The functions and powers of the regulating body would include:

- Conducting due diligence (gathering and evaluating information about the financial and technical capabilities of mining proponents);

- Requiring and assessing EIAs;

- Permitting/licensing; and

- Monitoring, compliance and enforcement.

The regulating body should also have the power to contract independent peer review of permitting/licensing applications and associated EIA. Funding of processing permit/licence applications and peer review should be borne by industry in accordance with 'user pays' principles.

The Working Group recognized that the creation and operation of such a regulating body would require significant resources and technical expertise. This expertise may not be currently found in smaller or developing States. Concerns were also expressed about multiple legislative instruments and institutions and lack of integration amongst them.

The Working Group concluded that a precedent existed, as well as clear benefits, for some administering functions of a regulating body to be delegated to a regional body or other third party. Any delegation would be exercised subject to the retention of sovereign decision-making power by the State or the States concerned. Articles 276 and 277 of UNCLOS foresees regional cooperation/integration for this type of activity.

The Working Group considered that delegating the function to a regional body or other third party would address existing gaps in national capacity; provide specialist expertise not found in-country; and avoid proliferation of national institutions, but would also seek to avoid the perception of bias and provides

checks and balances against undue influence and conflicts of interest.

Due diligence requirements

Due diligence has different legal meanings. Firstly, in the context of meeting international obligations to protect the marine environment there are due diligence requirements that States must satisfy in order to avoid liability for environmental damage. Incorporating the regulatory provisions detailed in this paper into national legislation would constitute one of the steps towards meeting due diligence requirements; another would consist of the effective implementation of the legislation. Secondly, in the context of deep seabed mining activities, due diligence requires an applicant for a licence to satisfy the decision-maker that they are a viable and responsible operator that is likely to comply with the State's regulatory requirements. For instance, before submitting an application for a DSM permit/licence within a national jurisdiction, an applicant would need to provide information on its financial and technical capabilities, relevant policies and procedures, and its plan of work. The State may also investigate the applicant's track record.

Allocation of mining sites

There are a number of methods of allocating sites for mining exploration, e.g. on a first-come first-serve basis, or through an auction/bidding process. The mechanism of allocation needs to be provided for in the Act. Allocation systems should enable investment by mining companies and facilitate competition. For example, they should provide for certainty of process, and prevent consideration of extraneous matters, such as trade competition effects.

The International Seabed Authority during its annual session

Permitting/licensing requirements and EIA

It was recognized that most deep seabed mineral projects are likely to have a significant impact on the environment. The permitting/licensing part of the Act should therefore incorporate provision for EIA, or should refer to existing national legislation that contains EIA requirements and processes. The existing legislation may also need to be amended in order to ensure that deep seabed mineral activities are appropriately covered by the existing EIA regime. Furthermore, an effects-based or impact-specific approach (rather than activity-specific approach) may also need to be adopted. This takes account of the possibility that some deep seabed scientific research and/or exploration activity may not have significant environmental impact, and that the capacity to mitigate adverse effects/impacts of certain activities will improve over time.

The permitting/licensing process consists of a recognized sequence of stages, including:

- Application for permit/licence, with supporting EIA;
- Public notification of application;
- Written submission on notified application;
- Public hearing of notified application;
- Decision; and
- Appeal process.

Industry representatives raised concerns about protecting the confidentiality of commercial information. The Working Group identified that there is a competing public policy issue of transparency and accountability. Balancing these two interests is important, and may be dealt with in the Act, if it is not already covered in existing legal instruments. The way the ISA Regulations deal with this is to provide for the issue of a general public notification that an application has been made without disclosing the exact coordinates of the prospecting/exploration area.

Applying principles in decision-making

The Working Group discussed some high-level principles and how they could be reflected in the Act, and incorporated into administrative decision-making. The Group chose to discuss the precautionary approach and best environmental practice.

Precautionary approach

The Working Group referred to Principle 15 of the Rio Declaration as a common starting point for defining the precautionary approach. Principle 15 states that:

> *"In order to protect the environment, the precautionary approach shall be widely applied by States according to their capabilities. Where there are threats of serious or irreversible damage, lack of full scientific certainty shall not be used as a reason for postponing cost-effective measures to prevent environmental degradation."*

Precaution may be defined as caution in advance, caution practised in the context of uncertainty, or informed prudence. The precautionary principle does not prevent activities with unknown effects/impacts from proceeding, but rather requires that they only proceed with appropriate checks and risk-reduction measures in place.

While the Rio Declaration precautionary principle uses the term "serious or irreversible damage", UNCLOS and the Authority's Mining Code employ the term "serious harm to the marine environment." Serious or irreversible damage, or serious harm to the marine environment, are thresholds that will be informed by scientific evidence. Nevertheless, the Working Group agreed it would be advantageous for the Act to provide a definition of these terms.

The qualifying words "according to their capabilities" used in the precautionary approach definition should not be used to justify a lower standard of due diligence. In the context of DSM, the burden of the precautionary approach falls on the entity making the application and undertaking the EIA. The State and its decision-making authority bear the responsibility of verification.

This is normally achieved through peer review of an EIA and monitoring of information supplied by the permit holder/licensee prior to and during the course of the mining operation.

The Working Group identified a need for more guidance on how to operationalize the precautionary approach in the context of DSM. The following examples of how the precautionary approach might be incorporated into decision-making were provided:

- Regular reporting of data on environmental impacts and pre-emptive action to avert serious harm to the marine environment.

- Ensuring the conservation of biodiversity through the creation of marine protected areas in proximity to the mining footprint; establishing corridors outside the mining areas and environmental compensation (i.e. protecting biodiversity of equal or greater value in a different location).

- Adopting an incremental test bed approach to a mining activity where impacts are uncertain, e.g. authorize test mining rather than immediately authorizing commercial-scale activity

The Working Group recommended that the Authority, or other competent authority, undertake technical consultations to operationalize the precautionary approach in the same manner that the Food and Agriculture Organization (FAO) has done with regard to deep sea fishing.

Best environmental practices

Best environmental practices – a requirement under international law in activities related to deep seabed minerals – generally refer to widely-accepted norms or customs of environmental and risk management. Where there is incomplete information and no established best practices, best environmental practice requires that the precautionary approach be applied.

Adaptive management is one example of the precautionary approach, and should form part of the Act. Adaptive management allows the proponent of a mining activity to fill the vacuum (where there is not an established practice) with a novel methodology. Adaptive management can be implemented by the mining operator through monitoring and assessing the

operator's activities, and by amending or improving the plan of work (including methods of mitigation) in cases where new information calls for a different approach.

Similarly, mining operators are obliged to satisfy best environmental practices and to provide the regulating authority with reporting/monitoring information confirming that best practices are being applied. The regulating authority is obliged to verify (either in-house or through independent peer review) that the information supplied by the mining operator confirms that it is adhering to best environmental practices. The Act should impose reporting requirements on the operator that will provide adequate information to the regulating authority to be able to meet this obligation. The terms of the Act should enable the regulating authority to retain sufficient control and flexibility within the permit/licensing model and to request amendments to the operator's conduct of activities.

Stages at which best environmental decision-making becomes relevant include, inter alia, the permitting/licensing phase, review of reporting/monitoring information, and in the case of any litigation.

One example of best environmental practices in the context of deep seabed mining would be to adopt a series of control strategies to protect the marine environment. The Working Group observed that best environmental practices will invariably be determined by the actual seabed mining activities in question and will be proportionate to their risk and scale.

Regional projects, such as the one currently managed by SPC, may assist States by identifying existing and proposing new guidelines so that a consistent approach is taken to decision-making. Examples of relevant guidelines include:

- The LTC's Guidelines in the Area;

- The Codes of Conduct issued by the International Marine Minerals Society and InterRidge;

- The Madang Guidelines.

The Act does not have to reflect the specifics of best environmental practice as long as the principle of best environmental practices is reflected as a statutory requirement. This enables best environmental practices to evolve over time and to adapt to specific scenarios.

Capacity-Building

In responding to calls for a regional approach to address issues relating to deep sea minerals in the Pacific Islands region, the European Union funded SPC Deep Sea Minerals Project that was established, aims to expand the economic resource base of Pacific ACP States by developing a viable and sustainable marine minerals industry. The Project's objective is to strengthen the system of governance and capacity of Pacific States in the management of deep sea minerals through the development and implementation of sound and regionally integrated legal frameworks, improved human and technical capacity and effective monitoring systems, through four key result areas:

- developing a regional legislative and regulatory framework for offshore minerals exploration and mining;

- assisting with the formulation of national policy, legislation and regulations within the 15 participating States;

- building national capacities;

- supporting the effective management and monitoring of offshore exploration and mining operations.

The SPC-EU Deep Sea Minerals Project is currently implemented in Cook Islands, Federated States of Micronesia, Fiji, Kiribati, Marshall Islands, Nauru, Niue, Palau, Papua New Guinea, Samoa, Solomon Islands, Timor Leste, Tonga, Tuvalu and Vanuatu. This four year Project (2011-2014) was launched in 2011.

Discussions during an SPC-EU Deep Sea Minerals Project meeting

Introduction

The level of current capacity in certain States and organizations to respond to, or initiate assessment of environmental impact, is inadequate for both the Area and EEZs. This lack of capacity and inadequate core competencies will severely restrict the ability of PICs to engage in, or manage potential impacts from DSM.

In determining capacity requirements, PICs need to consider the potential complexity and volume of work that might ensue. Some States have the potential within their EEZ for multiple tenements, while for others it may be a one-off or rare experience. The granting of exploration licences in the Area to two companies that are respectively sponsored by two PICs (i.e. Nauru and Tonga) have consolidated the call for institutional strengthening in PICs to enable them to respond appropriately to the challenges of this new industry.

Key areas for capacity-building identified by the working group include funding, competencies and training, knowledge management and regional cooperation.

Funding

Current funding models within the Authority are inadequate to meet the needs of managing and responding to EIAs and the monitoring, management and regulation of mining-related activities within the Area. Similarly, the ability of PICs to engage in (for the Area) or responding to EIAs (within EEZs) and the monitoring, management and regulation of mining-related activities is hampered by gaps in current assessment and management structures and processes. An evaluation and redesign of EIA and management-related fiscal structures is required to ensure adequate funds are available to both the ISA and PICs to effectively fulfil their international obligations and national responsibilities.

The group identified key areas/principles to ensure adequate funding;

- Proponent/contractor pays EIA-related costs (the Authority and PICs);

- Environmental management levies (the Authority);

- Membership fees (the Authority);

- Government allocation and commitment (PICs) could be derived from consolidated revenue, and in-kind assistance from regional entities, such as SPC;

- Development partners through bilateral and regional funding assistance (PICs).

Competencies and training

The LTC may require additional EIA skills and expertise to complement the range of skills and areas of expertise currently available within this committee. A subsidiary expert body of the LTC may be one way of expanding competencies within the current structure. The Authority should evaluate other options with Member States and other interested parties to expand EIA-specific competencies.

Within PICs there is significant disparity in their capacity to deal with mining issues. Countries where metalliferous mining occur have reasonable existing capacities to deal with mining issues while non-mining States have yet to develop EIA processes and supporting legislation and regulation. All States reported a general lack of capacity and a desire to increase in-country expertise in both assessing EIAs within the EEZ and conducting and assessing EIAs within the Area.

A dual EIA system (assessment) is supported where PICs concentrate on country-specific impacts, and outsource technical DSM-specific activities to external providers, with a preference for a strengthened regional body be mandated to perform this role. The advantages of such a system include improving national EIA-related skills without having to allocate scarce resources to developing DSM-specific skills for a one-off application or where a low number of applications will be received over many years. Further, this proposed model will address the ongoing issue of high professional turn over within the government system due to brain drain to the commercial sector and migration. Any outsourcing of technical assessment and advice falls with the competency of individual PICs who would retain sovereignty in all matters.

Training being received as a result of funding being provided by the ISA Endowment Fund. ©Rhodes Academy

A vital and shared area of concern was the need to develop and retain skills and ensure the transfer of skills within the region, countries and departments. Specific competency and training suggestions included:

- Full utilization of existing opportunities including:
  - The Authority has an Endowment Fund to provide both land-based and at-sea training. However, this scheme is currently poorly accessed by States as there was poor awareness of the scheme;
  - The University of the Sea (UOS) has established a programme that provides at-sea training for senior students and young researchers (although there is flexibility to include appropriate senior professionals);
  - Better coordination/awareness of existing/new training opportunities, i.e. University of the South Pacific (USP) and University of Papua New Guinea (UPNG).

- Additional training such as:
  - Seconded personnel from states/organizations that have skills that can be transferred to local personnel;
  - Apprenticeships/traineeships, knowledge transfer.

- Strengthen general EIA processes to ensure a transfer of EIA-related skills between non-DSM activities.

- Appropriate incentives provided to local companies to build capacity.

- Development of an external fund administered by a regional organization or the Authority, with contributions from a fee charged to contractors with each application.

- Strengthen a regional organisation (e.g. SPC) to effectively perform its technical and capacity building mandate.

- Retention pipeline. Knowledge/skill transfer and retention through:
  - Traineeships, apprenticeships (dual senior/junior positions);
  - Increase knowledge transfer post training and train the trainer activities; and
  - Adequate retention incentives.

Knowledge management

The lack of a regional comprehensive knowledge management system was identified as a significant obstacle to managing and responding to EIAs and the monitoring, management and regulation of DSM related activities within the Pacific region. While a number of databases exist they were seen as lacking compatibility and accessibility with narrow foci, such as marine minerals or fishing.

Sharing existing datasets via a central regional database was identified as a solution for effectively responding to DSM/EIA activities, as well as providing benefits to areas controlled by the Authority, PICs and regional environmental management. An expansion of the SOPAC Marine Minerals Database (to be developed under the SPC-EU Deep Sea Minerals Project) to include other relevant data was identified as a painless and cost-effective means of achieving this.

Key to the success of such a regional database would be the willingness of States and regional bodies to contribute data at a relevant scale (i.e. combined fish/mineral/environment data rather than individual boats). This could be overcome by strong leadership and direction from the PICs through appropriate regional bodies, and by establishing the database as a shared resource rather than one 'owned' by the body hosting it.

Similarly, support from the Authority, the SPC and the Regional Ocean Commissioner could contribute to the success of the regional comprehensive knowledge management system.

Regardless of the entity that will host the database, further discussions would be required regarding the funding and process of migrating existing data into a regional database. Volunteers were identified to assist in database design and funding, these include Paul Wilkes (IOC Samoa-Team Leader), Elaine Baker (UNEP/GRID-Arendal), Jan Steffen (IUCN), Yannick Beaudoin (UNEP/GRID-Arendal), Akuila Tawake (SPC) and the Authority.

The activities performed by the Commonwealth Scientific and Industrial Research Organisation (CSIRO) are a good example of an existing database that could be used as basis for a comprehensive regional knowledge management system.

Specific recommendations for the comprehensive regional knowledge management system included:

- A minimum compatible standard between existing regional databases;

- The central regional database should be user-friendly, accessible for data analysis/interrogation, updatable and provide metadata when available. It should also be accessible for compilations, be multi-layered and of a relevant scale; and

- It should adopt a holistic approach and incorporate a wide range of knowledge, including social and cultural knowledge.

Questions and observations to assist database design were also identified:

- Who are the end-users, resource managers in the individual States concerned?

- What type of data is required?

- What is the compatibility of database systems?

- What are the bathymetric data requirements?

- How can metadata and merging of existing databases be addressed?

- How to manage quality control of sampled data in both collection and compilation?

- Open source software should be preferred, although others, e.g. GIS, ARCGIS, MAPINFO, may be more appropriate?

- There are internet bandwidth issues in the region so access to the database could be a problem.

- What should be the area of coverage, should it include EEZs and/or areas between nations?

- It is essential to identify databases that could contribute to the central regional database.

- Which organization should manage the database?

- Should cultural knowledge and significance be incorporated?

Regional cooperation

Recognizing the benefits of cooperation and working through a regional body the group identified principles, structure, process/functions and a 'next steps' proposal. Principles were identified to guide both the Authority (currently the LTC) and a regional body. These principles included:

- Independence/neutrality;

- Knowledge-based that incorporates traditional and local knowledge with scientific data and findings;

- Integrated multi-stakeholder overview;

- Respect of jurisdictional responsibility and national sovereignty;

- Representative of 'the commons', state and ecological interests; and

- Implementation should be accomplished within an adequate timeframe as defined by responsible authority.

There was strong support for strengthening regional cooperation. It was envisaged that an existing body, e.g. SPC, could be strengthened to provide expert advice to States on EIA technical/DSM-related matters. It was noted that involving a regional organisation had the advantage of providing additional credibility to the decision-making process which may assist with any negative public perception regarding marine mining.

The regional body would be a semi-permanent, adaptive, user demand-based body that provides and supports the work of relevant experts on a case-by-case basis. Oversight could be achieved through existing representative structures. These activities would either be funded via existing programmes in the regional body, donor assistance or through effective EIA funding mechanism in PICs. This would develop a pool of national, regional and international experts to be drawn from government, international, academic/research institutions, private sector and civil society organizations.

Suggested activities for this regional body include:

- Development of a 'wish list' of all needs and preparation of a proposal for a realistic action plan;

- Consideration of possible alternatives to the EIA process which could be more valuable and appropriate in the region/jurisdiction of interest; and

- Use of DSM as a catalyst to consider consolidating or linking EIA for various ocean sectors.

The regional body would need to be legitimized and empowered by PICs with detailed terms of reference. The group resolved that a proposal should be put forward to a forthcoming SPC-SOPAC Division meeting which could explore the concept further.

In addition, a mandate could be given by PIC leaders to support the concept. This will require input from PICs in terms of what their needs and priorities are and options could be developed to address them.

Fauna on an undisturbed seamount © NIWA

Annex – List of Workshop Participants

SOPAC MEMBER COUNTRIES

Cook Islands

Mr Paul Lynch
Senior Legal Adviser (Seabed Minerals)
Office of the Deputy Prime Minister
PO Box 39
Rarotonga, Cook Islands
Tel: +682 29030/56388
Email: plynch.consulting@oyster.net.ck
blvilla1@oyster.net.ck

Mr Joseph Brider
Environment Officer
Te Ao Ora Natura · Biodiversity Conservation Unit
Puna Orama · Island Futures Division
PO Box 371
Rarotonga
Cook Islands
Ph: +682 21-256
Fax: +682 22-256
Email: joseph@environment.org.ck

Fiji Islands

Honorable Minister Timoci Lesi Natuva
Minister for Works and Public Utilities
Government of Fiji
Fiji Islands

Mr Malakai Finau
Director
Mineral Resources Department
Private Mail Bag
Suva, Fiji Islands
Tel: +679 338 1611
Mob: +679 990 4784
Fax: +679 337 0039
Email: malakai.finau@yahoo.com
m_finau@yahoo.com

Ms Namita Khatri
Acting Director Political and Treaties
Ministry of Foreign Affairs and International
Cooperation
Level 2, South Wing GCC Complex
87 Queen Elizabeth Drive,
Nasese, Suva Fiji.
Ph: (679) 323 9640
Fax: (679) 3301641
Email: nkhatri@govnet.gov.fj

Mr Ilai Waqa
Acting Manager Geological Surveys Division
Mineral Resources Department
Private Mail Bag
Suva, Fiji Islands
Tel: +679 3381611
Fax: +679 3370039
Email: ilai.waqa@mrd.gov.fj

Mr Venasio Nasara
Acting Manager
Mines Division
Mineral Resources Department
Private Mail Bag
Suva, Fiji Islands
Email: nasara@mrd.gov.fj

Ms Noleen Karan
Acting Deputy State Solicitor
Office of the Solicitor General
Level 7 Suvavou House
Suva, Fiji Islands
Ph: (679) 3309866(811)
Fax: (679) 3305421
Email: nkaran@govnet.gov.fj

Mr Wong Hen Loon
Senior Marine Geologist
Mineral Resources Department
Private Mail Bag
GPO Suva, Fiji Islands
Tel: +679 3381611
Fax: +679 3370039
Email: loona.wong@mrd.gov.fj

Mr Peni Suveinakama
Political and Treaties Officer
Ministry of Foreign Affairs
International Cooperation & Civil Aviation
PO Box 2200
Government Buildings
Suva, Fiji Islands
Tel: +679 323 9643
Fax: +679 331 7580
Email: peni.suveinakama@govnet.gov.fj

Ms Sereima Dovibua Koli
Acting Senior Scientific Officer
Environment Unit
Mineral Resources Department
Private Mail Bag
Suva, Fiji Islands
Tel: +679 3381611
Fax: 3370039
Email: sereima.dovibua@mrd.gov.fj

Mr Gene Waqanivalu Bai
Senior Legal Officer
Ministry of Foreign Affairs
PO Box 2213
Govt Buildings
Suva, Fiji Islands
Tel: +679 330 9866
Fax: +679 330 5421
Email: gene.bai@govnet.gov.fj

Kiribati

Mr Toani Takirua
Deputy Secretary (OIC)
Ministry of Fisheries and Marine Resources
Development
PO Box 64, Bairiki
Tarawa, Republic of Kiribati
Tel: +686 21099
Fax: +686 21120

Mr Tearinaki Tanielu
Geologist · Officer in Charge
Ministry of Fisheries and Marine Resources
Development
Minerals Unit
PO Box 64, Bairiki
Tarawa, Republic of Kiribati
Ph: +686 21099
Fax: +686 21120
Email: tearinaki@mfmrd.gov.ki

Marshall Islands

Honourable Mr John M. Silk
Minister of Foreign Affairs
PO Box 1349
Majuro, Marshall Islands 96960
Tel: (692) 625-318113012
Fax: (692) 625-4979
Email: isilk79@yahoo.com

Honourable Ms Amatlain E. Kabua
Ambassador
Embassy of the Republic of Marshall Islands
41 Borron Road
Suva, Fiji Islands
Tel: +679 338 7899
Fax: +679 338 7115
Email: ambassador@rmiembassyfiji.org

Mr Bernard Adiniwin
Assistant Secretary
Bureau of Multilateral Affairs
Ministry of Foreign Affairs
PO Box 1349
Majuro, Marshall Islands 96960
Tele: (692) 625-318113012
Fax: (692) 625-4979
Email: bemardadiniwin@gmail.com

Nauru

Mr Bryan Starr
Director of Environment
Department of Commerce Industry & Environment
Yaren District, Republic of Nauru
Tel: +674 444 3133
Email: bryan.star@naurugov.nr

Mr Michael Aroi
Acting Secretary
Department of Foreign Affairs and Trade
Yaren District, Republic of Nauru
Central Pacific
Tel: +674 557 3040
Email: michael.aroi@naurugov.nr

Papua New Guinea

Ms Lyndah Brown-Kola
Technical Manager
Mineral Resources Authority
PO Box 1906
Port Moresby 121, NCD
Papua New Guinea
Tel: +675 321 3511
Fax: +675 321 5311
Email: lbkola@mra.gov.pg

Mr Jerry Naime
Manager – Exploration Coordination
Mineral Resources Authority
PO Box 1906
Port Moresby 121, NCD
Papua New Guinea
Tel: +675 321 3511
Fax: +675 321 0189
Email: jnaime@mra.gov.pg

Mr Gregory Roaveneo
Assistant Director – Policy Advisory Branch
Department of Mineral Policy & Geohazards
Management
Boroko NCD
Port Moresby, Papua New Guinea
Tel: +675 321 4238
Email: gregory_roaveneo@mineral.gov.pg

Tonga

Mr Asipeli Palaki
Director
Ministry of Environment and Climate Change
PO Box 917
Nuku'alofa, Tonga
Tel: +676 8887999
Fax: 25 · 057
Email: apalaki@gmail.com

Ms Kate McPherson
Environment Legislation Policy Officer
Ministry of Environment and Climate
Change
PO Box 1074
Nuku'alofa, Tonga
Tel: +676 8427127
Email: katemcpherson@iinet.net.au

Tuvalu

Mr Kakee Pese Kaitu
Permanent Secretary
Ministry of Natural Resources
Vaiaku, Funafuti
Tuvalu
Ph: (+688) 20160 (office)
Mob: (+688) 900 888
Email: kkaitu@gov.tv
kpkaitu@yahoo.com.au

Mr Avafoa Irata
Deputy High Commissioner
Tuvalu High Commission
16 Gorrie St
Suva, Fiji
Tel: (679) 3301355
Fax: (679) 3308479
Email: avafoairata@yahoo.com

Vanuatu

Mr Brooks Rakau
Minerals Coordinator
Department of Geology, Mines & Water
Resources
Private Mail Bag 9001
Port Vila, Vanuatu
Tel: +678 22423
Fax: +678 22213
Email: brakau@vanuatu.gov.vu

Mr Christopher Ioan
Director/Commissioner of Mines
Department of Geology, Mines & Water
Resources
Private Mail Bag 9001
Port Vila, Vanuatu
Tel: +678 22423
Fax: +678 22213
Email: cioan@vanuatu.gov.vu

INTERNATIONAL & REGIONAL AGENCIES

Commonwealth Scientific and Industrial Research Organization (CSIRO)

Mr Raymond Binns
Honorary Fellow
CSIRO
272 Elssmore Rd
Exeter, NSW 2579
Australia
Tel: +612 48836069
Email: entex@acenet.com.au

Mr Nic Bax
Senior Research Scientist
CSIRO Wealth from Oceans Flagship
CSIRO Marine Laboratories
GPO Box 1538
Hobart TAS 7001
Australia
Tel: 03 6232 5341
Fax: 03 6232 5485
Email: nic.bax@csiro.au

International Union for Conservation of Nature (IUCN)

Mr Jan Henning Steffen
Regional Marine Program Coordinator
International Union for Conservation of
Nature (IUCN)
Private Mail Bag
5 Ma'afu Street
Suva, Fiji Islands
Tel: +679 9382722
Fax: +679 310 0128
Email: jan.steffen@iucn.org

Pacific Islands Forum Secretariat (PIFS)

Ms Linda Kaua
Economic Reform Officer
Pacific Islands Forum Secretariat
Private Mail Bag
Suva, Fiji Islands
Tel: +679 331 2600 (Ext 2251)
Fax: +679 322 0249
Email: lindak@forumsec.org.fj

Secretariat of the Pacific Regional Environment Programme (SPREP)

Mr Tim Carruthers
Coastal and Marine Adviser
SPREP
PO Box 240
Apia, Samoa
Ph: +685 21929 (Ext 264)
Email: timc@sprep.org

Following with same address as above:

Mr Trevor Durbin
Intern
Email: trevord@sprep.org

UNEP/GRID-Arendal

Mr Yannick Beaudoin
Head of Marine Division
UNEP/GRID-Arendal
Postboks 183
N-4802 Arendal
Norway
Tel: +47 9542 9247
Fax: +47 3703 5050
Email: Yannick.Beaudoin@grida.no

Ms Elaine Baker
UNEP/GRID-Arendal
The University of Sydney
NSW 2006, Australia
Tel: +612 9351 3000
Fax: +612 9351 0184
Email: ebaker@usyd.edu.au
Elaine.baker@sydney.edu.au

NATIONAL INSTITUTIONS

China Ocean Mineral Resources R & D Association (COMRA)

Mr Jiancai Jin
Director
COMRA
1 Fuxingmenwai Ave, Beijing 100860
People's Republic of China
Tel: +86 (10) 68030504
Fax: +86 (10) 68030504
Email: jin@comra.org

Following with same address as above:

Mr Jun Jiang
Engineer
Tel: +86 (10) 68047767
Fax: +86 (10) 68047767
Email: jjun@comra.org

Deep Ocean Resources Development Co Ltd. (DORD)

Mr Akira Tsune
Geologist
Exploration Department
DORD
1-3-15 Nihonbashi-Horidome-Cho
Chuoh-ku, 103-0012
Japan
Tel: 81-3-5614-7212
Fax: 81-3-3664-1930
Email: tsune@dord.co.jp

Duke University

Mr Linwood Pendleton
Director of Ocean & Coastal Policy
Duke University
135 Duke Marine Lab Road
Beauford, NC 28516
United States of America
Tel: +1 805 794 8206
Email: linwood.pendleton@duke.edu

German Federal Institute for Geosciences and Natural Resources

Ms Annemiek Vink
Biogeologist
German Federal Institute for Geosciences and Natural Resources
Geozentrum Hannover
Stilleweg 2
30 655 Hannover, Germany
Tel +49 (0)511 6432392
Fax +49 (0)511 643532353
Email: Annemiek.Vink@bgr.de

Japanese Agency for Marine-Earth Science and Technology (JAMSTEC)

Mr Kazuhiro Kitazawa
Special Adviser to the Director
JAMSTEC (Japanese Agency for Marine Earth Science and Technology)
2-15 Natsushima, Yokosuka 237-0061
Japan
Tel: +81 (0)46-867-9191
Fax: +81 (0)46-867-9195
Email: kitazawa@jamstec.go.jp

Japan Oil, Gas and Metals National Corporation (JOGMEC)

Mr Tetsuhiko Toyohara
Senior Researcher
JOGMEC
2-10-1 Toranomon, Minato-ku,
Tokyo, Japan
Phone: +81-3-6758-8452
Fax: +81-44-520-8730
Email: toyohara-tetsuhiko@jogmec.go.jp

Korea Ocean Research & Development Institute (KORDI)

Mr Jang Wan Bang
Secretary
KORDI Minerals (South Pacific) Ltd
2nd Floor, Downtown Blvd
PO Box 16881
Suva, Fiji Islands
Tel: +679 330 7678/990 8701
Fax: +679 330 7678
Email: ratu88fj@hotmail.com

Mr Kiseong Hyeong
Principal Research Scientist
Deep-Sea & Marine Georesources Research Department
KORDI
1787 Haeanlo, Ansan 426-944
Korea
Tel: 82-31-400-6382
Fax: 82-31-418-8772
Email: kshyeong@kordi.re.kr

Mr Hyeon Su Jeong
Team Leader
Seafloor Sulphides R&D Organisation
KORDI
Ansan PO Box 29
Seoul 425-600, Korea
Tel: +82 31 500 4582
Fax: +82 31 500 4584
Email: jeonghs@kordi.re.kr

Minerals Policy Institute

Mr Charles Roche
Executive Director
Mineral Policy Institute
PO Box 6043
Gurrawheen, Australia
Tel: +61 89343 0151
Email: charles.roche@mpi.org.au

National Institute of Water & Atmospheric Research (NIWA)

Mr Malcolm Clark
Principal Scientist (Deepwater Fisheries)
NIWA
Private Bag 14-901
Wellington 6241
New Zealand
Tel: +64 4 386 0300
Fax: +64 4 386 0574
Email: malcolm.clark@niwa.co.nz

Pennsylvania State University

Mr Charles (Chuck) Fisher
Professor of Biology
208 Mueller Laboratory
The Pennsylvania State University
University Park, PA 16802
United States of America
Tel: +1 814 865 3365
Fax: +1 814 865 9131
Email: cfisher@psu.edu

Research GNS Science

Mr Ian Graham
Director Research
GNS Science (Geological and Nuclear Sciences)
91 Fraser Avenue, Johnsonville
Wellington 5040
New Zealand
Tel: 644 5704677
Fax: 644 5704657
Email: i.graham@gns.cri.nz

U.S. Geological Survey

Mr James Hein
Senior Scientist
U.S. Geological Survey
121 Hollywood Ave
Santa Cruz, CA 95060
United States of America
Tel: +1 650-329-5287
Fax: +1 650-329-5299
Email: jhein@usgs.gov

University of Wollongong

Ms Robin Warner
Australian National Centre for Ocean Resources
and Security
University of Wollongong
PO Box 324
Mittayong NSW 2575
Australia
Tel: +614 23951853
Email: rwarner@uow.edu.au

Mr Steve Raaymakers
PhD Candidate – Deep Sea Mining
University of Wollongong
PO Box 968
Edge Hill 4870
Australia
Tel: +6140 9909 422
Email: steve@eco-strategic.com

PRIVATE SECTOR & CIVIL SOCIETY

Anindilyakwa Land Council

Mr Ross McDonald
Mining and Environment Advisor
Anindilyakwa Land Council
PO Box 386
Alyangula WT 0885
Australia
Tel: (08) 8987 4008
Fax: (08) 8987 4099
Mob: 0429 854 697
Email: rmcdonald@alcnt.com.au

Fiji Environmental Law Association

Ms Kiji Vukikomoala
Coordinator
Fiji Environmental Law Association
15 Ma'afu Street
c/o IUCN Private Mail Bag
Suva, Fiji Islands
Tel: +679 331 9084/7080997
Fax: +679 310 0128
Email: kiji.vukikomoala@fela.org.fj

GeoPacific Limited

Mr Tausia Kerto
Country Manager
GeoPacific Limited
PO Box 9975
Nadi Airport, Fiji Islands
Tel: +679 672 7150
Fax: +679 672 7152
Email: tausia@geopacific.com.au

Mr Steven Whitehead
Exploration Manager
GeoPacific Ltd
Lot 3, Brewer Rd, Martintar
Fiji Islands
Tel: +679 6727150
Email:
steven.whitehead@geopacific.com.au

Howards Lawyers

Ms Akanisi Nabalarua
Solicitor
Howards Lawyers
Level 7, FNPF Place
Victoria Parade, GPO Box 13687
Suva, Fiji Islands
Tel: 777 2495
Fax: 3300180
Email: anabalarua@howardslaw.com.fj

Nauru Ocean Resources Inc. (NORI)

Mr Robert Heydon
Vice President
Nauru Ocean Resources Inc (NORI)
88 Stanmere St, Brisbane QLD
Australia, 4152
Tel: +614 00767300
Email: rgh@nauruoceanresources.com

Nautilus Minerals

Mr Paula Taumoepeau
Tonga Country Manager
Nautilus Minerals Inc and TOML
Nuku'alofa, Tonga
Tel: +676 21733
Fax: +676 21734
Email: pmt@nautilusminerals.com

Ms Samantha Smith
Environment & Community Manager
Nautilus Minerals
PO Box 1213
Milton, Qld 4064
Australia
Tel: +617 3318 5555
Fax: +617 3318 5500
Email: sls@nautilusminerals.com

Neptune Minerals

Mr Daniel Alberdi, Jr
Environmental Manager
Neptune Minerals, Inc
5858 Central Avenue
St. Petersburg, Florida
USA 33707
Tel: (727) 897-5542
Mob: (813) 716-5266
Email: danny.alberdi@neptuneminerals.com

Mr Tim McConachy
SVP Science & Exploration
Neptune Minerals, Inc.
14 Barrackburn Rd, Pymble
NSW 2075
Australia
Tel: +61 417818390
Email:
tim.mcconachy@neptuneminerals.com

Mr Harvey Cook
SVP Regional Affairs
Neptune Minerals, Inc.
41 Black Street
Brighton Vic 3186
Australia
Email: harvey.cook@neptuneminerals.com

North South Environmental Law

Mr Robert Makgill
Director
North South Environmental Law
Lev 3, 60 Parnell Rd
Parnell, New Zealand
Tel: +649 304 0043
Fax: +649 303 2427
Email: RMakgill@nsenvironmentallaw.com

Pacific Reach Ltd

George & Sangeeta Rubine
Pacific Reach Limited
Suva, Fiji Islands
Tel: +679 327 0181
Mob: +679 992 3853
Fax: +679 327 0182
Email: virgo@connect.com.fj
Fiji Times Office

Ms Repeka Nasiko
Reporter
Fiji Times
Lautoka, Fiji Islands
Tel: +679 9919808
Email: rnasiko@fijitimes.com.fj

Planning Solutions Inc.

Mr Charles Morgan
Senior Environmental Planner
Planning Solutions Inc.
210 Ward Avenue, Suite 330
Honolulu HI 96814
USA
Tel: 808-550-4539
Fax: 808-550-4549
Email: cmorgan@psi-hi.com

INTERNATIONAL SEABED AUTHORITY

Mr Nii Odunton
Secretary General
International Seabed Authority
14-20 Port Royal Street
Kingston, Jamaica
Tel:+1 876 922 9105
Fax:+1 876 922 0159
Email: nodunton@isa.org.jm

Following with same address as above:

Mr Michael Lodge
Deputy to the Secretary-General
Email: mlodge@isa.org.jm

Mr Adam Cook
Scientific Affairs Officer
Phone: +1·876·922·9105·9 (x288)
Fax: +1·876·967·0801
Email: ACook@isa.org.jm

Ms Anna Elaise
Webmaster/Publications Officer
Email: annae@isa.org.jm

SOPAC DIVISION/SECRETARIAT OF THE PACIFIC COMMUNITY

Mr Russell Howorth
Director
SPC
SOPAC Division/SPC
Secretariat of the Pacific Community
Private Mail Bag, GPO
Suva, Fiji Islands
Tel: +679 338 1377
Fax: +679 337 0040
Email: russell@sopac.org

Following with same address as above:

Mr Akuila Tawake
Team Leader – Deep Sea Minerals Project
Email: akuila@sopac.org

Ms Hannah Lily
Legal Adviser – Deep Sea Minerals Project
Email: hannah@sopac.org

Ms Vira Atalifo
Project Assistant – Deep Sea Minerals Project
Email: vira@sopac.org

Ms Laisa Baoa
Travel and Conference Coordinator
Email: laisa@sopac.org

Ms Emily Artack
Maritime Boundaries Project Officer
Email: emily@sopac.org

Ms Emily Moli
Pacific Way Reporter

Mr Joji Nabalarua
Senior Cameraman & Editor
SPC

Mr Daryl Woo
IT Officer
Email: daryl@sopac.org

Mr Enele Gaunavou
Clerk/Driver
Email: enele@sopac.org

www.ingramcontent.com/pod-product-compliance
Lightning Source LLC
Chambersburg PA
CBHW052043190326
41520CB00002BA/171

9 789768 241047